I0569317

Foundations of the Kingdom of God

This is volume 1 of a six-book series on the Kingdom of God.

Book Series

Preface

From the first words of Jesus' ministry—"The Kingdom of God has come near"—to the final vision of Revelation where heaven and earth are renewed, the Scriptures resound with a single, unifying theme: God's reign breaking into our world.

Yet for many, the Kingdom of God remains a mystery. Some imagine it as a distant heaven, far removed from daily life. Others reduce it to a personal spiritual experience. But Jesus spoke of the Kingdom as a present reality—God's rule and reign reshaping, transforming human lives, communities, and even creation itself. The Kingdom is not just a future hope; it is a present invitation.

This series of books is born out of that conviction. Each volume explores a different dimension of the Kingdom of God—its biblical foundations, its expression in the life and teaching of Jesus, its impact on personal discipleship, its shaping of community, its engagement with the wider world, and its ultimate fulfillment in God's new creation.

The Kingdom of God is not abstract theology; it is the heartbeat of the gospel. It challenges us to rethink our values, reimagine our communities, and rediscover the hope that God is making all things new. On the seventh day of creation, God rested, but The Creator was not finished with creating. The Creator called all of creation to participate in the creative work, The Creator called us. This series is written for seekers, students, and disciples who long for a deeper understanding of the gospel Jesus preached—and who desire to live in light of it.

My prayer is that these books will help you see Scripture with fresh eyes, recognize the presence of God's reign in your own life, and join in the Spirit's work of building communities of love, justice, and hope. Together, may we hear anew the words of Jesus:

"Seek first the Kingdom of God and His righteousness."

Table Of Content

Foundations of the Kingdom

"When God began to create the heavens and the earth," (Genesis 1:1, NRSVue)

"The Lord has established his throne in the heavens, and his kingdom rules over all." (Psalm 103:19, NRSVue)

"How beautiful upon the mountains are the feet of the messenger who announces peace, who brings good news, who announces salvation, who says to Zion, "Your God reigns."" (Isaiah 52:7, NRSVue)

Chapter 1

Why the Kingdom Matters

I sometimes smile when I think about how quickly we Christians can get distracted. We'll argue about church programs, fret over doctrinal fine print, or even split entire denominations over details of polity. And yet, if you open the Gospels, Jesus seems remarkably focused on one thing: *the Kingdom of God.* It was the heartbeat of his preaching, the substance of his parables, and the frame of his prayers. If the Kingdom mattered that much to Jesus, surely it should matter to us. But what do we actually mean by it?

The Kingdom in Scripture's Story

From the earliest pages of Scripture, God's reign is woven into the narrative. The Psalms sing it again and again: *"The Lord is king forever and ever; the nations shall perish from his land"* (Ps 10:16, NRSVue). Israel's poets and prophets clung to this confession not as abstract theology but as survival. In exile, when empires rose and fell, this conviction gave them hope. Walter Brueggemann describes such testimony as "an act of resistance against the dominant claims of empire," a refusal to concede that Babylon or Rome had the last word (Brueggemann, *Theology of the Old Testament*, 1997, p. 579).

Think also of Exodus: the liberation of slaves from Egypt was not only about freedom from Pharaoh's brick quotas, but about allegiance to a new ruler. *"The Lord will reign forever and ever"* (Exod 15:18). The Kingdom was not a distant heaven but a new social reality—God's people reshaped under God's rule.

7

Isaiah carries this thread into poetry: *"The people who walked in darkness have seen a great light"* (Isa 9:2). Here divine kingship is not about domination but illumination. In the ancient Near East, kings were often depicted as bearers of light, reflecting divine favor and cosmic order. Israel subverted this imagery: true light does not emanate from a human throne but from the presence of God. Ellen Davis observes that Isaiah's vision is as agricultural as it is political—the light makes crops grow, children flourish, and nations find peace (Davis, *Scripture, Culture, and Agriculture*, 2009, pp. 65–66).

Kingdom as Covenant and Comfort

The Kingdom matters because it frames covenant. The Exodus was not just an escape route—it was an invitation into relationship. God's reign is expressed in Torah, in justice for the widow and orphan, in sabbath rest for the land. Terence Fretheim argues that this covenantal sovereignty is inherently relational, where God's power is expressed not through coercion but accompaniment (Fretheim, *God and World in the Old Testament*, 2005, p. 121).

This covenantal dimension also gives the Kingdom emotional depth. When the psalmist prays, *"The Lord is my shepherd"* (Ps 23:1), he is not reciting doctrine but remembering covenant presence in the valley of shadows. Dallas Willard once remarked that the Kingdom is simply "the range of God's effective will"—wherever God's will is done (Willard, *The Divine Conspiracy*, 1998, p. 25). That means the shepherd's comfort, the prophet's fire, and the exile's hope all belong to the same Kingdom reality.

Why It Resonates with Us

The Kingdom also matters because it touches something deeply human. We all long for order in chaos, for light in darkness, for a community that knows justice. The prophets sang of it, Jesus embodied it, and communities today still enact it—sometimes through Eucharist, sometimes through protest marches, sometimes through shared meals.

Walter Wink insists that the Kingdom is God's confrontation with "the Powers"—those social and spiritual systems that idolize wealth, domination, and violence (Wink, *Naming the Powers*, 1984, pp. 7–8). Gustavo Gutiérrez pushes further: the Kingdom is good news for the poor precisely because it dismantles the structures that keep them poor (Gutiérrez, *A Theology of Liberation*, 1971, pp. 103–04). In this way, Kingdom language is not only spiritual consolation but social revolution.

And yet, it also takes on tender, artistic hues. Augustine described the Kingdom as the place where "our hearts rest in God" (*Confessions*, I.1). Martin Luther spoke of God's reign as a gracious rule breaking into ordinary lives through faith. I find that the Kingdom is best glimpsed not in arguments about it but in stories—in the light of a candle lit at a vigil, in a child laughing at the communion table, in a farmer who lets his field lie fallow in sabbath trust.

Modern Parallels

Communities today still echo this ancient imagery of Kingdom through ritual, art, and storytelling. African American spirituals sang of freedom in coded Kingdom language: "Go Down, Moses" was Exodus set to rhythm. Latin American base communities read Scripture together as a political act, embodying the reign of God in barrios and villages (Howard-Brook, *The Church Before Christianity*, 2001, pp. 212–13). Even in our own local congregations, when bread is broken and stories are shared, the Kingdom is there—small as a mustard seed, but alive.

Why It Matters Now

So why does the Kingdom matter? Because without it, the gospel shrinks. If we reduce faith to personal morality or church membership, we miss the vast sweep of God's reign. The Kingdom gives us a horizon larger than our private anxieties. It reminds us that God's justice is bigger than our politics, God's mercy deeper than our failures, God's light stronger than our darkness.

And maybe, just maybe, if we keep our eyes open, we'll see what Isaiah saw—the great light dawning even in our own neighborhoods.

Chapter 1 - Sources

- Augustine. *Confessions*. Trans. Henry Chadwick. Oxford: Oxford University Press, 1991.

- Brueggemann, Walter. *Theology of the Old Testament: Testimony, Dispute, Advocacy*. Minneapolis: Fortress, 1997.

- Davis, Ellen. *Scripture, Culture, and Agriculture: An Agrarian Reading of the Bible*. Cambridge: Cambridge University Press, 2009.

- Fretheim, Terence. *God and World in the Old Testament: A Relational Theology of Creation*. Nashville: Abingdon, 2005.

- Gutiérrez, Gustavo. *A Theology of Liberation*. Maryknoll: Orbis, 1971.

- Howard-Brook, Wes. *The Church Before Christianity*. Maryknoll: Orbis, 2001.

- Willard, Dallas. *The Divine Conspiracy: Rediscovering Our Hidden Life in God*. San Francisco: HarperOne, 1998.

- Wink, Walter. *Naming the Powers: The Language of Power in the New Testament*. Philadelphia: Fortress, 1984.

- Wright, N.T. *How God Became King: The Forgotten Story of the Gospels*. San Francisco: HarperOne, 2012.

- *Anchor Yale Bible Dictionary*. 6 vols. New York: Doubleday, 1992.

- NRSVue Bible

Chapter 2

In the Beginning: God the King

Whenever I return to Genesis, I find myself slowing down. These opening chapters are not just ancient history—they are poetic overtures, full of mystery and promise. The Bible doesn't begin with arguments about God's existence. It begins with God's reign. *"In the beginning when God created the heavens and the earth..."* (Gen 1:1, NRSVue). Creation is not random; it is ordered, purposeful, and—most importantly—ruled by the One who speaks it into being.

This is why the Kingdom cannot be tacked on later in Scripture as if it were a new idea Jesus invented. It is already here in the opening cadence of creation. The Kingdom is not something God had to "come up with" after the fall—it is the framework of reality itself.

Creation as God's Kingdom

The very act of creation introduces us to God as King. Unlike the chaotic, violent cosmogonies of Israel's neighbors—where gods battle monsters to carve out space—Genesis tells a different story. With a word, God separates light from darkness, land from sea, chaos from cosmos. John Goldingay notes that Genesis "presents God's sovereignty as quiet and unquestioned," unlike the noisy combat myths of Babylon (*Old Testament Theology*, 2003, p. 67).

This is no small theological shift. Ancient Mesopotamian texts like the *Enuma Elish* portray creation as the spoils of war: the god Marduk slays the sea-dragon Tiamat and fashions the world out of her carcass. By contrast, Genesis insists there is no rival to the Creator. God reigns without resistance. As Karl Barth observed, "Creation is the kingdom of God in embryo, the theater where His sovereignty first takes form" (*Church Dogmatics*, III.1, p. 87).

The repeated refrain, *"And God saw that it was good,"* is not filler—it is a royal decree. In the ancient Near East, kings would issue proclamations of peace and stability. Genesis echoes this pattern but universalizes it: the King's decree covers light, seas, birds, beasts, and even humankind. The world itself is the King's temple, every corner resonating with divine order. Augustine called this the *"first sermon of creation"*—that before we even hear a prophet, the heavens declare God's glory (*Confessions*, XI.4).

Humanity as Image-Bearers

If creation reveals God as King, humanity is portrayed as royal stewards. *"Let us make humankind in our image, according to our likeness; and let them have dominion…"* (Gen 1:26). In the ancient Near East, kings placed statues of themselves in conquered lands to mark their authority. Genesis redefines that practice: every human being becomes a living image, a signpost of divine reign.

This was—and still is—radical. The poor farmer, the refugee woman, the shepherd boy, the merchant—all bear God's image, not just the ruling elite. Bonhoeffer reflected that the *imago Dei* means humanity is free "for God" and "for others," never for domination (*Creation and Fall*, 1937, p. 62). In this sense, dominion does not mean exploitation but responsibility. N.T. Wright explains that to bear God's image is to be a "royal priesthood," reflecting God's wise rule into creation and offering creation's worship back to God (*Surprised by Scripture*, 2014, p. 68). The point is not domination but vocation: humanity is invited to partner with God in cultivating the flourishing of the earth. Calvin echoes this when he describes creation as a theater of God's glory, where humans act as stewards on stage, not owners behind the curtain (*Institutes*, I.14.20).

This explains why the Sabbath concludes creation's rhythm. Rest is not laziness; it is alignment with God's reign. Ellen Davis beautifully remarks that sabbath is "God's royal signature" on creation, a reminder that we live not by endless labor but by divine generosity (Davis, *Scripture, Culture, and Agriculture*, 2009, p. 83). In the Sabbath command we hear both theology and politics: God, not Pharaoh, determines the rhythm of life.

The Rejection of God's Kingship

Of course, Genesis also tells us how quickly we resist this vocation. The story of the fall (Gen 3) is not simply about eating forbidden fruit—it is about humanity's refusal to live under God's reign. To reach for the tree of knowledge was to grasp at sovereignty, to declare: *we will be our own kings*.

Walter Brueggemann observes that this primal disobedience is "a revolt against creatureliness," an attempt to secure autonomy apart from covenant (*Genesis*, Interpretation, 1982, p. 45). The result is not liberation but exile, a fracturing of relationships—with God, with one another, with the earth itself.

The pattern continues. Cain resents his brother and sheds blood (Gen 4). Lamech boasts of seventy-sevenfold vengeance (Gen 4:24). The flood narrative portrays a world consumed by violence (Gen 6). And the Tower of Babel shows humanity uniting not in worship but in self-exaltation. Rather than scattering to steward creation, they build a monument to their own rule. Karl Barth once quipped that Babel is "humanity's first ecumenical council"—a parody of unity that refuses God's reign (*Church Dogmatics*, III.1, p. 183).

Comfort in the King's Presence

And yet, the biblical story does not end with rebellion. Even in Genesis, God's reign is not withdrawn. After exile from Eden, God clothes the humans with garments (Gen 3:21)—a small but profound act of royal compassion. When Cain is condemned, God places a mark of protection upon him (Gen 4:15). Judgment and mercy intertwine, reminding us that divine kingship is not ruthless tyranny but patient, covenantal care.

This balance of sovereignty and mercy becomes Israel's foundation. Psalm 24 echoes Genesis when it declares: *"The earth is the Lord's and all that is in it, the world, and those who live in it"* (Ps 24:1). The cosmos is not ownerless—it belongs to the King who made it. For Israel, this was comfort as much as command. They belonged to a ruler who created out of love.

As George Eldon Ladd emphasizes, the Kingdom is not only about rule but relationship—it is "the dynamic reign of God breaking into history for salvation" (*The Presence of the Future*, 1974, p. 54). Genesis offers a foretaste: a King who reigns not to crush but to cultivate.

Modern Parallels: Creation as Kingdom Witness

How might we hear this today? In a world where we often confuse ownership with value, Genesis reminds us that the earth is not ours to exploit. Sabbath practices—letting land rest, releasing debts, honoring limits—remain prophetic acts of Kingdom living.

Think of communities practicing sustainable agriculture in the spirit of Jubilee. Or of churches where shared gardens feed the neighborhood. Or of rituals that draw on creation imagery—water poured in baptism, bread broken in Eucharist, oil poured in anointing. All of these are reminders that God's Kingdom began in a garden, not a palace.

Art and storytelling also echo Genesis. Howard-Brook notes how grassroots Christian communities often narrate their faith in agricultural metaphors—soil, seed, harvest—because these embody the rhythms of Kingdom life (*The Church Before Christianity*, 2001, p. 97). In poetry and song, believers rediscover creation not as backdrop but as testimony.

I think of the Taizé community in France, where worship often includes chants like *"In the Lord I'll be ever thankful."* The simplicity of song, silence, and prayer in a garden chapel feels like Eden reimagined. It's a reminder that the Kingdom does not begin in cathedrals of stone but in gardens, meals, and shared rest.

Why Genesis Still Matters

The Kingdom matters from the very beginning because creation itself is testimony. To confess God as King is to remember that life is not an accident, that our vocation is not self-invention, and that our deepest rest is found not in striving but in sabbath trust.

When we read Genesis with open eyes, we find more than a creation story. We find a Kingdom manifesto: a God who rules not by violence but by speaking life, a humanity called to mirror divine care, and a world that still whispers, in every sunrise and sabbath, *"The Lord reigns."*

Chapter 2 - Sources

- Augustine. *Confessions*. Trans. Henry Chadwick. Oxford: Oxford University Press, 1991.

- Barth, Karl. *Church Dogmatics*, Vol. III.1. Edinburgh: T&T Clark, 1958.

- Brueggemann, Walter. *Genesis*. Interpretation Commentary Series. Atlanta: John Knox Press, 1982.

- Davis, Ellen. *Scripture, Culture, and Agriculture: An Agrarian Reading of the Bible*. Cambridge: Cambridge University Press, 2009.

- Goldingay, John. *Old Testament Theology*. Vol. 1. Downers Grove: IVP Academic, 2003.

- NRSVue Bible.

- Wright, N.T. *Surprised by Scripture: Engaging Contemporary Issues*. New York: HarperOne, 2014.

Chapter 3

Covenant and Calling

One of the most important truths about the Kingdom of God is this: it does not emerge in isolation. God doesn't simply reign in the abstract. God reigns through a people who are called, shaped, and sent. The story of the Kingdom is, at its heart, a story of covenant.

From Promise to People

Genesis does not linger in universal abstractions for long. By chapter 12, the narrative narrows to one man, Abram. *"Go from your country and your kindred and your father's house to the land that I will show you. I will make of you a great nation, and I will bless you, and make your name great, so that you will be a blessing"* (Gen 12:1–2, NRSVue).

Notice the pattern: call, promise, purpose. Abram is not chosen for privilege but for responsibility—*so that you will be a blessing.* This covenant is the seedbed of the Kingdom: God's reign embodied in a people who exist for the sake of the world.

N.T. Wright insists that this covenant is not a detour but the central way God establishes His reign in history: "God's plan to rescue creation itself was to work through a people" (Wright, *How God Became King*, 2012, p. 103). The Kingdom is personal, but it is never private. It always unfolds communally.

Exodus: The Politics of Liberation

If Genesis 12 plants the seed, Exodus waters it with liberation. God hears the cry of the oppressed and responds: *"Let my people go, so that they may worship me"* (Exod 9:1). This is not just deliverance—it is a transfer of allegiance. Pharaoh loses his grip; Yahweh claims His people.

Walter Brueggemann calls the Exodus "the primal narrative of Israel's identity," a story that announces God's reign as liberation over against empire (Brueggemann, *The Prophetic Imagination*, 1978, p. 25). For enslaved people, this was not abstract theology. It was survival. It was hope. It was God as King breaking the chains of Pharaoh's kingdom.

Dietrich Bonhoeffer, writing under the shadow of Hitler, understood this with piercing clarity: "The Kingdom of God is not a realm of ideas but of reality, where God takes the side of the oppressed" (Bonhoeffer, *Ethics*, 1949, p. 65). To confess God as King is to recognize Pharaoh's days are numbered.

Sinai: The Covenant of Belonging

Liberation is only the beginning. At Sinai, God binds this newly freed people into covenant. The Ten Commandments are not abstract moral laws—they are a charter for a Kingdom community. The prologue makes this clear: *"I am the Lord your God, who brought you out of the land of Egypt, out of the house of slavery"* (Exod 20:2).

Law flows from liberation, not the other way around. Covenant is not about earning God's reign but embodying it. As Ellen Davis reminds us, Torah is "instruction for a distinctive way of life," not a burden but a gift (Davis, *Getting Involved with God*, 2001, p. 118).

Here, the Kingdom takes social shape. Sabbath rest is mandated not only for Israel but for servants, animals, and even the land (Exod 20:10; Lev 25:4). The poor are to be protected, the widow and orphan provided for. The reign of God is manifest in justice, mercy, and shared rest.

Israel's Vocation: Blessed to Bless

Covenant always points outward. Israel is not chosen to hoard blessing but to extend it: *"I will bless you...so that you will be a blessing...in you all the families of the earth shall be blessed"* (Gen 12:2–3).

Gustavo Gutiérrez presses this point: "Election is not about separation but mission, not about superiority but service" (Gutiérrez, *A Theology of Liberation*, 1971, p. 107). To belong to the covenant is to bear responsibility for the flourishing of others.

And yet, Israel often forgot this. The temptation to privatize blessing, to collapse covenant into nationalism or religion, was constant. The prophets arose to remind them: covenant is not a privilege but a vocation. Amos thundered: *"You only have I known of all the families of the earth; therefore I will punish you for all your iniquities"* (Amos 3:2). To be chosen is to be accountable.

Covenant as Kingdom Pattern

Here we see the pattern that runs through all of Scripture:

- God calls a people.
- God liberates them.
- God binds them in covenant.
- God sends them to embody His reign for the sake of the world.

John Calvin captured it well: "the covenant of God is the bond of the Kingdom" (Calvin, *Institutes*, II.10.2). The Kingdom is never just an idea of rule; it is the lived reality of a people under covenant, reflecting the justice and mercy of their King.

Why Covenant Still Matters

In our modern world, we often reduce faith to individual spirituality. "My personal relationship with Jesus" can sound almost like a private contract. But the Kingdom of God does not work that way. It is always covenantal, always communal, always for the sake of the world.

We see glimpses of this in communities that take covenant seriously: churches practicing radical hospitality, congregations sharing their resources, movements standing in solidarity with the marginalized. These are modern echoes of Sinai and Abraham's call—a covenant people embodying the reign of God.

Conclusion

The Kingdom matters because covenant matters. From Abraham's tent to Sinai's thunder, from liberation to law, God reigns through a people. Chosen not to dominate, but to bless. Called not to privilege, but to responsibility. Saved not for escape, but for mission.

The covenant story is our story, too. We belong to a Kingdom not built on conquest but on covenant love. And through us, God still longs to bless the nations.

Chapter 3 - Sources

- Wright, *How God Became King*, 2012, p. 103.
- Brueggemann, *The Prophetic Imagination*, 1978, p. 25.
- Bonhoeffer, *Ethics*, 1949, p. 65.
- Davis, *Getting Involved with God*, 2001, p. 118.
- Gutiérrez, *A Theology of Liberation*, 1971, p. 107.
- Calvin, *Institutes of the Christian Religion*, II.10.2.

Chapter 4

God's Reign in Israel's Story

When Israel told its story, it didn't begin with kings or priests. It began with a God who liberates, a God who commands justice, a God who reigns. The Kingdom of God is not an invention of Jesus or the church; it is the heartbeat of Israel's life. To follow their story is to see the contours of divine kingship traced through liberation, law, worship, and prophetic vision.

Exodus: God as Liberator and King

At the Red Sea, Israel discovered what it meant to belong to a new King. The hymn of Exodus 15 declares: *"The Lord will reign forever and ever"* (Exod 15:18, NRSVue). In the ancient world, kings boasted of military victories; here, the God of slaves defeats Pharaoh's army with wind and sea. Walter Brueggemann calls this "the most important single act of divine sovereignty in Israel's memory" (*Theology of the Old Testament*, 1997, p. 173).

Exodus is not just escape from slavery; it is enthronement of God as King. Dietrich Bonhoeffer, preaching in 1933, drew the connection directly: "God is not just a distant ruler. God reigns where the cries of the oppressed are heard, and where chains are broken" (*Creation and Fall*, 1937, p. 78). To belong to God is to be free from Pharaoh. The Kingdom begins in liberation.

Sinai: The Shape of Kingdom Life

The Exodus leads to Sinai. Freedom without form easily dissolves into chaos. At Sinai, God gives Torah, not as an arbitrary law code, but as a covenant charter. The prologue makes this clear: *"I am the Lord your God, who brought you out of the land of Egypt, out of the house of slavery"* (Exod 20:2). Law flows from liberation.

Ellen Davis insists that Torah is not a burden but a gift: "instruction for a distinctive way of life" (*Getting Involved with God*, 2001, p. 118). Sabbath rest is mandated not only for Israel but for servants, animals, and even the land (Exod 20:10; Lev 25:4). The Kingdom is manifest in the rhythms of justice and rest.

This stands in stark contrast to Pharaoh's kingdom of endless brick quotas (Exod 5:6–18). Walter Wink notes that Israel's sabbath is "a protest against the Powers" (*Engaging the Powers*, 1992, p. 99). To rest is to declare that God, not empire, determines the rhythm of life.

Israel's Desire for a Human King

And yet, Israel struggled with the invisible reign of God. In 1 Samuel 8, the elders demand: *"Appoint for us a king to govern us, like other nations"* (1 Sam 8:5). Samuel warns them: kings will take their sons, daughters, fields, and flocks. But the people insist.

John Goldingay observes that Israel's request reflects a deeper anxiety: "It is easier to trust a visible throne than the elusive sovereignty of God" (*Old Testament Theology*, 2003, p. 201). The irony is rich: in seeking to be like other nations, Israel forgets that their very vocation was to be different.

God concedes, but reluctantly: *"They have not rejected you, but they have rejected me from being king over them"* (1 Sam 8:7). The monarchy becomes a paradox—on one hand, David is celebrated as the anointed shepherd-king (2 Sam 7); on the other, every king after him is measured against God's own reign. As Karl Barth put it, "the monarchy of Israel is tolerated, not willed, as a witness to the monarchy of God" (*Church Dogmatics*, II.1, p. 370).

Worship: The Kingdom in Liturgy

Even while kings ruled, Israel's worship insisted that God alone reigned. The Psalms proclaim: *"The Lord is king; let the earth rejoice*" (Ps 97:1). These enthronement psalms served as liturgical declarations that no human throne could rival God's sovereignty.

Augustine read the psalms as a way of shaping communal identity: "When we sing 'The Lord is king,' it is not poetry but reality—our voices confess the reign under which we live" (*Expositions on the Psalms*, Ps. 96). Worship became Israel's act of resistance, reminding them who their true King was, even in exile.

Prophets: Kingdom as Justice and Righteousness

When kings forgot covenant, the prophets rose to remind them. Isaiah envisioned a reign where justice and peace would embrace: *"For a child has been born for us...his authority shall grow continually, and there shall be endless peace for the throne of David and his kingdom"* (Isa 9:6–7).

Amos cut more sharply: *"Let justice roll down like waters, and righteousness like an ever-flowing stream"* (Amos 5:24). Obery M. Hendricks Jr. notes that Amos challenges not only personal piety but structural injustice, making Kingdom language inherently political (*The Politics of Jesus*, 2006, p. 42).

For Jeremiah, the Kingdom was about shepherding: *"Woe to the shepherds who destroy and scatter the sheep of my pasture"* (Jer 23:1). God promised a righteous Branch who would execute justice. George Eldon Ladd argued that these prophetic visions planted the expectation of a future Kingdom that is both divine and restorative (*The Presence of the Future*, 1974, p. 110).

The Kingdom Pattern in Israel's Story

If we trace Israel's narrative, we see a recurring pattern:

- Liberation from oppression.
- Covenant as a way of life.
- Temptation to trust human kings.
- Worship that insists God alone reigns.
- Prophets calling the people back to justice.

This is the Kingdom in Israel's story. Always contested, always fragile, but always anchored in the conviction: *"The Lord reigns forever; your God, O Zion, for all generations"* (Ps 146:10).

Why This Story Matters Now

Israel's story is not just ancient history—it is our story. We, too, are tempted to place our trust in visible thrones: governments, markets, leaders who promise security. We, too, forget Sabbath and drift back into Pharaoh's quotas of endless production. And we, too, need prophets who remind us that the Kingdom is measured in justice, mercy, and righteousness.

The reign of God is not nostalgic theology; it is a living reality. When churches practice Sabbath economics, when worship proclaims God's sovereignty over nationalism, when prophets speak truth to power—the story of Israel's God continues.

And in this story, we prepare for the One who will embody the Kingdom fully—the child of Isaiah's vision, the Branch of Jeremiah's hope, the shepherd-king who will feed his flock.

Chapter 4 - Sources

- Brueggemann, Theology of the Old Testament, 1997, p. 173.
- Bonhoeffer, *Creation and Fall*, 1937, p. 78.
- Davis, *Getting Involved with God*, 2001, p. 118.
- Wink, *Engaging the Powers*, 1992, p. 99.
- Goldingay, *Old Testament Theology*, 2003, p. 201.
- Barth, *Church Dogmatics*, II.1, p. 370.
- Augustine, *Expositions on the Psalms*, Ps. 96.
- Hendricks, *The Politics of Jesus*, 2006, p. 42.
- Ladd, *The Presence of the Future*, 1974, p. 110.

Chapter 5

The Prophets and the Coming Kingdom

If Israel's story teaches us anything, it's that memory is fragile. Freed from Pharaoh, Israel soon longed for the leeks of Egypt. Gifted Torah, they drifted into idolatry. Entrusted with kings, they found themselves seduced by power. At every turn, God raised up prophets—those inconvenient voices who would not let the people forget.

The prophets did not invent the Kingdom; they reminded Israel of it. They spoke of covenant fidelity, justice for the vulnerable, and a hope that stretched beyond exile toward a future reign of God that would heal the world.

Prophets as Voices of Covenant Faithfulness

The prophets were not fortune-tellers but covenant enforcers. Walter Brueggemann insists that their role was "to re-describe the world as though YHWH were truly King" (*The Prophetic Imagination*, 1978, p. 13). They diagnosed Israel's forgetfulness and called the people back to God's reign.

Think of Micah's simplicity: *"What does the Lord require of you but to do justice, and to love kindness, and to walk humbly with your God?"* (Mic 6:8). This is covenant life in shorthand. Terence Fretheim emphasizes that the prophets located God's reign in ordinary relationships—economics, agriculture, courts, and care for the poor (*God and World in the Old Testament*, 2005, p. 142).

Themes of Justice and Righteousness

The prophetic refrain was always the same: God's Kingdom is measured by justice and righteousness. Amos, speaking from the periphery of power, announced: *"Let justice roll down like waters, and righteousness like an ever-flowing stream"* (Amos 5:24).

Obery M. Hendricks Jr. argues that such declarations make the prophets political theologians, insisting that divine sovereignty always has social consequences (*The Politics of Jesus*, 2006, p. 39). Isaiah sharpened the image: *"Ah, you who join house to house, who add field to field, until there is room for no one but you"* (Isa 5:8). Land greed, economic exploitation, and false worship all became signs of a kingdom at odds with God's reign.

Ellen Davis observes that the prophets often rooted their visions in agrarian imagery—fields, vineyards, rain, rivers—because the health of the land was bound to the health of the people (*Scripture, Culture, and Agriculture*, 2009, p. 119). Justice was not abstract; it was whether the widow harvested grain, whether the poor ate bread, whether the land itself was kept in sabbath rest.

Prophetic Imagination and Hope

Even as they judged, the prophets dared to hope. Isaiah saw a day when *"nation shall not lift up sword against nation, neither shall they learn war any more"* (Isa 2:4). Ezekiel envisioned dry bones rising, animated by the Spirit (Ezek 37:4–6). Jeremiah promised a new covenant written on hearts (Jer 31:31–34).

Brueggemann calls this the "prophetic imagination," the ability to envision alternatives to empire and despair (*Prophetic Imagination*, 1978, p. 40). George Eldon Ladd notes that such visions birthed the eschatological hope of Israel, where the Kingdom was not only present but awaited in fullness (*The Presence of the Future*, 1974, p. 110).

For exiles in Babylon, these promises were lifelines. John Goldingay observes that prophetic hope did not deny suffering but re-narrated it: exile was not the end, but a stage in the drama of God's reign (*Old Testament Theology*, 2003, p. 355).

The Messianic Horizon

Out of this prophetic hope emerged the expectation of a Messiah—a king anointed not for conquest but for justice. Isaiah sang of a child born to reign with peace: *"His authority shall grow continually, and there shall be endless peace for the throne of David and his kingdom"* (Isa 9:7).

Jewish tradition carried this hope as an ache and a promise. N.T. Wright suggests that the prophets seeded a vision of God's reign that was "already breaking in through justice, but awaiting consummation in a final deliverance" (*Jesus and the Victory of God*, 1996, p. 204).

The prophets, in other words, kept the Kingdom alive during centuries of disappointment. They dared to say: God still reigns, God still promises, and God still intends to set the world right.

Why the Prophets Still Speak

Prophets were not just voices for their own time; they still confront us today. They remind us that worship without justice is hollow (Amos 5:21–24). They warn us against kingdoms of greed and violence. They urge us to imagine alternatives to endless war, exploitation, and despair.

Walter Wink believed that the prophetic word was indispensable because it unmasks the Powers that demand our allegiance (*Naming the Powers*, 1984, p. 95). The prophets expose our Pharaohs and Babylons and point us again to God's reign.

And perhaps most importantly, they teach us to hope. They train our imagination for a Kingdom not yet fully here, but already glimpsed in every act of justice, every word of truth, every song of resistance.

Conclusion

The Kingdom of God in the prophets is both warning and promise. It is a call to remember covenant, to practice justice, to resist empire. And it is a vision of a future where swords are beaten into plowshares, bones rise from graves, and God's reign brings peace.

If we listen carefully, the prophets are still speaking. They remind us that the Kingdom is not a private dream but a public reality. It is not nostalgia but promise. It is not yet complete—but it is on the way.

Chapter 5 - Sources

- Brueggemann, *The Prophetic Imagination*, 1978, p. 13.
- Fretheim, *God and World in the Old Testament*, 2005, p. 142.
- Hendricks, *The Politics of Jesus*, 2006, p. 39.
- Davis, *Scripture, Culture, and Agriculture*, 2009, p. 119.
- Brueggemann, *The Prophetic Imagination*, 1978, p. 40.
- Ladd, *The Presence of the Future*, 1974, p. 110.
- Goldingay, *Old Testament Theology*, 2003, p. 355.
- Wright, *Jesus and the Victory of God*, 1996, p. 204.
- Wink, *Naming the Powers*, 1984, p. 95.

Chapter 6

The Kingdom Breaks In

If the prophets left Israel with one burning hope, it was this: God would not leave the world as it was. Exile was not the end. Empire was not final. A Messiah would come, and with him, God's reign would be revealed in full. By the time of the New Testament, this expectation had become the heartbeat of Jewish faith. And into this climate walked a fiery preacher on the banks of the Jordan River.

John the Baptist: Preparing the Way

John's cry was stark and urgent: *"Repent, for the kingdom of heaven has come near"* (Matt 3:2, NRSVue). He dressed like Elijah (2 Kgs 1:8), quoted Isaiah (Isa 40:3), and confronted power without apology. His baptism was not just ritual cleansing; it was a preparation for a new world order under God's reign.

N.T. Wright argues that John's ministry signaled "the turning of the ages," a prophetic act declaring that God's promises were at last breaking in (Wright, *Jesus and the Victory of God*, 1996, p. 161). Walter Brueggemann would call this a moment of "rupture"—the old narratives of power giving way to God's alternative (Brueggemann, *Prophetic Imagination*, 1978, p. 41).

John's message was both warning and hope: judgment for the unrepentant, mercy for the humble. His call to repentance was not about private guilt but about allegiance. To repent was to turn from the kingdoms of Caesar and Herod and pledge loyalty to the reign of God.

Jesus' Proclamation: The Kingdom Has Come Near

When Jesus begins his ministry, the continuity with John is clear. Mark records his first words: *"The time is fulfilled, and the kingdom of God has come near; repent, and believe in the good news"* (Mark 1:15).

Here the Kingdom is not a distant promise but a present reality. George Eldon Ladd called this the "already/not yet" of the Kingdom—the reign of God inaugurated in Jesus' life and ministry, but awaiting final fulfillment (*The Presence of the Future*, 1974, p. 120).

The Greek word *engiken* ("has come near") implies immediacy: the reign of God is not postponed to heaven but breaking into history. John Calvin described this moment as "the very presence of God's dominion, displayed in the Son" (*Institutes*, II.15.4).

The Kingdom as Present and Future

One of the greatest tensions in Jesus' teaching is this paradox: the Kingdom is already here, and yet it is still to come.

- Already: *"If it is by the finger of God that I cast out the demons, then the kingdom of God has come to you"* (Luke 11:20).
- Not yet: *"Your kingdom come. Your will be done, on earth as it is in heaven"* (Matt 6:10).

Dallas Willard explained it as "the range of God's effective will," which is expanding now, but will only be complete when heaven and earth are made new (*The Divine Conspiracy*, 1998, p. 25).

This paradox is not a problem but a gift. It keeps us from both despair and triumphalism. We do not give up, because the Kingdom has already come. But we do not presume it is finished, because the Kingdom is not yet complete.

Signs of the Kingdom

How does Jesus demonstrate the nearness of the Kingdom? Not through political campaigns or military conquest, but through acts of healing, liberation, and restoration. The blind see, the lame walk, the lepers are cleansed, the poor hear good news (Matt 11:5).

Walter Wink insisted that these miracles were not suspensions of natural law but signs that "a new order of reality had entered history" (*Engaging the Powers*, 1992, p. 107). They were enactments of God's reign over disease, demons, and despair.

Even the choice of disciples reflected this Kingdom. Fishermen, tax collectors, zealots—an unlikely coalition embodying God's new society. Dietrich Bonhoeffer called discipleship "the visible form of the Kingdom in the world" (*Discipleship*, 1937, p. 47). To follow Jesus was to step into the reality of God's reign.

The Clash of Kingdoms

Of course, to proclaim God's reign was to challenge every rival reign. Jesus' announcement of the Kingdom was not spiritually neutral. It threatened Rome, Herod, the temple establishment, and even the demonic powers that haunted the margins.

Obery Hendricks Jr. reminds us that Jesus' Kingdom message was profoundly political: "To call God king is to call Caesar not" (*The Politics of Jesus*, 2006, p. 52). No wonder the Gospels portray constant conflict—exorcisms, debates, confrontations. Wherever the Kingdom advanced, resistance followed.

Karl Barth put it bluntly: "The Kingdom of God is the abolition of all kingdoms that stand against it" (*Church Dogmatics*, IV.2, p. 96). The cross would become the ultimate collision point.

Why It Matters

When we hear Jesus say, *"The kingdom of God has come near,"* we are not listening to an ancient slogan. We are hearing the announcement that God's reign is breaking into our world. The question is not whether the Kingdom is real—it is whether we will recognize it.

The Kingdom is already here in every act of mercy, every stand for justice, every moment when God's will is done on earth as in heaven. And it is still to come, drawing us into hope, patience, and longing.

The prophets prepared us. John announced it. Jesus embodied it. And now, the question presses on us: will we live as citizens of this Kingdom, even while other thrones still claim our loyalty?

Chapter 6 - Sources

- Wright, *Jesus and the Victory of God*, 1996, p. 161.
- Brueggemann, *Prophetic Imagination*, 1978, p. 41.
- Ladd, *The Presence of the Future*, 1974, p. 120.
- Calvin, *Institutes of the Christian Religion*, II.15.4.
- Willard, *The Divine Conspiracy*, 1998, p. 25.
- Wink, *Engaging the Powers*, 1992, p. 107.
- Bonhoeffer, *Discipleship*, 1937, p. 47.
- Hendricks, *The Politics of Jesus*, 2006, p. 52.
- Barth, *Church Dogmatics*, IV.2, p. 96.

Chapter 7

The Signs of the Kingdom

Jesus did not only preach the Kingdom—he enacted it. His words and his works were inseparable. Wherever he healed the sick, fed the hungry, cast out demons, or forgave sins, the Kingdom was not simply explained; it was demonstrated. These "signs" were not parlor tricks to prove divinity. They were flashes of God's reign breaking into the world.

Healing as Kingdom Power

The Gospels place healing at the heart of Jesus' ministry. Lepers are cleansed (Mark 1:41), paralytics walk (Mark 2:11), blind eyes open (Mark 10:52). Each act is more than compassion—it is proclamation. George Eldon Ladd argued that "the miracles of Jesus are the powers of the age to come, breaking into this present evil age" (*The Presence of the Future*, 1974, p. 149).

In the ancient world, sickness carried not only physical suffering but social exclusion. Lepers were isolated, the blind often forced to beg, women with bleeding conditions barred from worship. Healing restored not only bodies but communities. Ellen Davis calls this "the social dimension of healing," where the Kingdom is revealed as wholeness for both the person and the body of God's people (*Getting Involved with God*, 2001, p. 129).

Dallas Willard suggested that Jesus' healings reveal "a universe drenched with God's power," where the natural and spiritual are never truly separate (*The Divine Conspiracy*, 1998, p. 33).

Exorcisms: The Kingdom Against the Powers

If healing restores bodies, exorcism confronts the deeper bondage of evil. When Jesus casts out demons, the crowds marvel: *"With authority and power he commands the unclean spirits, and out they come!"* (Luke 4:36).

For Walter Wink, exorcisms expose the clash of kingdoms: God's reign colliding with the "Powers" that enslave human life (*Naming the Powers*, 1984, p. 32). These stories are not primitive superstition but theological theater—signs that in Jesus, the dominion of darkness is giving way to the dominion of light.

N.T. Wright emphasizes that exorcisms revealed "Israel's God reclaiming sovereignty over creation, expelling forces that had usurped his rule" (*Jesus and the Victory of God*, 1996, p. 192). Each deliverance was a preview of the cosmic victory yet to come.

Feeding the Hungry: The Economics of the Kingdom

The feeding of the five thousand (Mark 6:30–44) is not just a miracle of multiplication; it is a parable in action. Jesus provides bread in the wilderness, echoing the manna of Exodus (Exod 16). Here is God's Kingdom economy: abundance shared freely, no one turned away, twelve baskets of surplus.

Gustavo Gutiérrez interprets such miracles as signs of liberation, challenging systems that create scarcity amid plenty (*A Theology of Liberation*, 1971, p. 114). When Jesus tells his disciples, *"You give them something to eat"* (Mark 6:37), he invites them into Kingdom participation: to trust God's abundance and to embody it in generosity.

Forgiveness as a Sign of the Kingdom

Perhaps the most radical sign of the Kingdom was forgiveness. When Jesus declared to the paralytic, *"Son, your sins are forgiven"* (Mark 2:5), the religious leaders cried blasphemy. Forgiveness was God's prerogative—and that was the point. In Jesus, God's reign was not a future courtroom but a present grace.

Karl Barth wrote that forgiveness is "the royal prerogative of God's reign, whereby sin is dethroned and grace enthroned" (*Church*

Dogmatics, IV.1, p. 223). Dietrich Bonhoeffer agreed: "Forgiveness is the breaking in of the Kingdom of God into the world of sin" (*Discipleship*, 1937, p. 46).

Forgiveness reconstitutes communities as much as it heals consciences. To forgive was to announce that exile was ending, debts were being released, and God's reign of mercy was taking hold.

The Signs as Sacraments of the Kingdom

Taken together, these signs—healings, exorcisms, feedings, forgiveness—were sacraments of the Kingdom: visible realities of God's invisible reign. They were not ends in themselves but windows into a deeper truth.

John Calvin described miracles as "seals of the Kingdom," confirming that God's promises were being enacted in real time (*Institutes*, I.8.9). They were not spectacles to dazzle but sacraments to reveal.

And they were also warnings. Jesus insisted that to see miracles without perceiving the Kingdom was blindness. *"If I by the finger of God cast out demons, then the kingdom of God has come upon you"* (Luke 11:20). To witness a sign was to be confronted with a choice: align with God's reign, or resist it.

Why the Signs Still Matter

Modern readers sometimes stumble over the miracles. Did they really happen? Can we explain them scientifically? But to fixate on mechanics is to miss the point. The signs of the Kingdom are not about explaining how, but proclaiming who. They reveal a God who reigns not from a distance but in embodied compassion, liberation, and restoration.

Even today, the Kingdom still breaks in through signs. Every time the sick are cared for, the oppressed set free, the hungry fed, the sinner forgiven—the Kingdom is enacted. The church's sacraments, acts of justice, and works of mercy all continue this pattern. As Augustine put it, "What we now celebrate in symbol, God will one day reveal in fullness" (*Sermon 272*).

Conclusion

The signs of the Kingdom remind us that God's reign is not only proclaimed but performed. In Jesus, words became deeds, sermons became suppers, promises became power.

The Kingdom is not just an idea to believe—it is a reality to be encountered. And if we pay attention, we may still see its signs: a life restored, a community reconciled, a meal shared, a word of forgiveness spoken. These are not small things. They are fragments of eternity breaking into time.

Chapter 7 - Sources

- Ladd, *The Presence of the Future*, 1974, p. 149.
- Davis, *Getting Involved with God*, 2001, p. 129.
- Willard, *The Divine Conspiracy*, 1998, p. 33.
- Wink, *Naming the Powers*, 1984, p. 32.
- Wright, *Jesus and the Victory of God*, 1996, p. 192.
- Gutiérrez, *A Theology of Liberation*, 1971, p. 114.
- Barth, *Church Dogmatics*, IV.1, p. 223.
- Bonhoeffer, *Discipleship*, 1937, p. 46.
- Calvin, *Institutes of the Christian Religion*, I.8.9.
- Augustine, *Sermon 272*.

Chapter 8

The Kingdom in Parables

Jesus was a master storyteller. He could disarm with a single sentence, disturb with a short tale, and invite his listeners into a reality they did not expect. The parables are not moral fables or children's stories. They are provocations—puzzles designed to reorient imagination around the Kingdom of God.

Why Parables?

When the disciples asked why he taught in parables, Jesus answered: *"To you has been given the secret of the kingdom of God, but for those outside, everything comes in parables"* (Mark 4:11, NRSVue). The parables both reveal and conceal. They invite the faithful into deeper understanding while unsettling those who cling to conventional wisdom.

C.H. Dodd famously called parables "weapons of warfare" in the battle of ideas—short stories that tease the mind into active thought (*The Parables of the Kingdom*, 1935, p. 16). N.T. Wright adds that Jesus' parables "were not illustrations, but announcements of a new reality" (*Jesus and the Victory of God*, 1996, p. 229). They were not meant to make things simple but to open space for transformation.

The Mustard Seed and Yeast: The Small Becomes Great

"The kingdom of heaven is like a mustard seed... the smallest of all the seeds, but when it has grown it is the greatest of shrubs" (Matt

13:31–32). Or again: *"The kingdom of heaven is like yeast that a woman took and mixed with three measures of flour until all of it was leavened"* (Matt 13:33).

These parables subvert expectations. In the ancient world, kingship was associated with power, spectacle, and grandeur. Here Jesus insists the Kingdom begins in hidden, humble ways. Walter Brueggemann calls this "the scandal of small beginnings" (*Texts Under Negotiation*, 1993, p. 72). The reign of God does not arrive with armies but with a seed, a pinch of yeast, an act of quiet faithfulness.

Dallas Willard suggests that these images invite us to trust the slow, steady work of God's reign—even when it seems insignificant (*The Divine Conspiracy*, 1998, p. 41).

The Hidden Treasure and the Pearl: Joyful Surrender

"The kingdom of heaven is like treasure hidden in a field, which someone found and hid; then in his joy he goes and sells all that he has and buys that field" (Matt 13:44). Or like a merchant who sells everything for a pearl of great value (Matt 13:45–46).

Here the Kingdom is not duty but delight. Its worth eclipses all else. Augustine reflected: "To find the Kingdom is to find that for which the soul was made; all else is small by comparison" (*Sermons on Selected Lessons of the New Testament*, Sermon 34).

Dietrich Bonhoeffer sharpened the edge: "When Christ calls a man, he bids him come and die" (*Discipleship*, 1937, p. 79). To embrace the Kingdom is costly—but the cost is joyfully borne for the sake of what is found.

The Prodigal Son: The Kingdom of Mercy

Few parables disclose the Kingdom more vividly than the story of the prodigal son (Luke 15:11–32). A younger son squanders his inheritance, only to be embraced by a father who runs to meet him.

This is not simply a story about repentance; it is a revelation of the reign of mercy. Karl Barth described it as "the parable of the Father's Kingdom, where forgiveness is the order of the day" (*Church Dogmatics*, IV.3.1, p. 408).

Obery Hendricks Jr. notes that the older brother embodies the temptation to turn covenant into exclusion: to hoard blessing rather than extend it (*The Politics of Jesus*, 2006, p. 113). But in the Kingdom, both the prodigal and the resentful elder are summoned to the banquet of grace.

Parables as Kingdom Invitations

Taken together, the parables disclose several themes:

- The Kingdom begins small but grows beyond expectation.
- The Kingdom is of surpassing worth, worth giving everything to obtain.
- The Kingdom is about mercy, reconciliation, and welcome.
- The Kingdom overturns assumptions of power, wealth, and exclusion.

They are not merely stories to entertain but invitations to live differently. John Dominic Crossan once quipped that parables are "lures for transformation" (*In Parables*, 1973, p. 15).

Why Parables Still Matter

The parables remind us that God's reign rarely looks like we expect. It comes as a seed, a pearl, a banquet, a forgiving father. They force us to wrestle with uncomfortable questions: Do we trust small beginnings? Do we treasure the Kingdom above all? Do we rejoice when mercy offends our sense of fairness?

These are not ancient riddles; they are present challenges. Every time we hear a parable, we are placed in the story. Are we the prodigal, the older brother, the seed sower, the hidden treasure seeker? The Kingdom breaks in not just when we understand the parable, but when we live inside it.

Conclusion

Through parables, Jesus taught that the Kingdom of God is hidden yet powerful, costly yet joyful, merciful yet unsettling. They invite us to imagine a world reordered by God's reign and to step into that imagination with our lives.

The Kingdom is not an abstraction. It is a mustard seed in the soil, yeast in the dough, a father running down the road. The question is whether we will have ears to hear—and the courage to enter the story.

Chapter 8 - Sources

- Dodd, *The Parables of the Kingdom*, 1935, p. 16.
- Wright, *Jesus and the Victory of God*, 1996, p. 229.
- Brueggemann, *Texts Under Negotiation*, 1993, p. 72.
- Willard, *The Divine Conspiracy*, 1998, p. 41.
- Augustine, *Sermons on Selected Lessons of the New Testament*, Sermon 34.
- Bonhoeffer, *Discipleship*, 1937, p. 79.
- Barth, *Church Dogmatics*, IV.3.1, p. 408.
- Hendricks, *The Politics of Jesus*, 2006, p. 113.
- Crossan, *In Parables*, 1973, p. 15.

Chapter 9

The Cross and the Crown

No symbol of the Kingdom is more paradoxical than the cross. In the Roman world, the cross was not a decoration or religious icon. It was an instrument of terror, a public billboard announcing that Caesar was king and rebels would be crushed. Yet the early church dared to proclaim that on the cross, Jesus was enthroned. The ultimate tool of empire became the throne of God's reign.

Crucifixion as Political Theater

Roman crucifixion was carefully staged. Victims were stripped, mocked, and displayed as warnings. Martin Hengel described crucifixion as "a political and military punishment" intended to humiliate and intimidate (*Crucifixion*, 1977, p. 86). It was Rome's way of saying: *this is what happens when you challenge the empire.*

The Gospels underscore this political theater. Jesus is robed in purple, crowned with thorns, hailed in mockery: *"Hail, King of the Jews!"* (Mark 15:18, NRSVue). The irony is not lost. What Rome intended as ridicule becomes revelation. Karl Barth wrote that "in the passion of Christ, the sovereignty of God is exercised in its deepest humiliation" (*Church Dogmatics*, IV.1, p. 223).

The Cross as Enthronement

John's Gospel makes the point explicit. Jesus is "lifted up" (John 3:14; 12:32)—a phrase that means both exaltation and crucifixion. On

Golgotha, Jesus is enthroned as King. The inscription above his head, *"Jesus of Nazareth, King of the Jews"* (John 19:19), meant mockery to Pilate but proclamation to the church.

N.T. Wright insists that the cross is "the kingdom of God in action, enthroned love defeating the world's powers" (*The Day the Revolution Began*, 2016, p. 358). George Eldon Ladd adds that Jesus' death was not the failure of the Kingdom but its decisive in-breaking: "The victory of the Kingdom is revealed in weakness" (*The Presence of the Future*, 1974, p. 193).

Dietrich Bonhoeffer, facing his own martyrdom, grasped this deeply: "The cross is not the end of the Kingdom, but its beginning" (*Letters and Papers from Prison*, 1953, p. 109).

The Powers Disarmed

Paul saw the cross as the moment when the "powers and principalities" were stripped of their authority: *"He disarmed the rulers and authorities and made a public example of them, triumphing over them in it"* (Col 2:15).

Walter Wink explained this as the exposure of the Powers: "The cross unmasks their idolatry, revealing that their claim to ultimate power is a lie" (*Engaging the Powers*, 1992, p. 151). Rome did its worst, and yet God's Kingdom was not defeated but revealed.

John Calvin wrote that Christ "triumphed over Satan and all the hosts of hell" not by force but by "the wondrous paradox of weakness" (*Institutes*, II.16.7). In this inversion, the cross becomes the crown.

The Cross as Kingdom Ethics

But the cross is not only Christ's victory—it is also the pattern for his followers. *"If any want to become my followers, let them deny themselves and take up their cross and follow me"* (Mark 8:34).

Bonhoeffer captured it in a single line: "When Christ calls a man, he bids him come and die" (*Discipleship*, 1937, p. 79). The Kingdom is not advanced by coercion but by self-giving love. Augustine echoed this when he described the church as "a people shaped by the love of God, even to contempt of self" (*City of God*, XIV.28).

Here the ethic of the Kingdom is unveiled: victory through surrender, greatness through service, life through death.

Why the Cross Matters

The cross is not merely a doctrine of personal salvation—it is the decisive act of God's reign. It reveals that the Kingdom does not operate like the kingdoms of this world. Caesar rules by the sword; Christ reigns by the cross.

To confess the crucified one as King is to declare that power is redefined, that love is stronger than violence, that forgiveness is the true revolution. It is to see the crown in the cross.

Conclusion

At the cross, we see the deepest mystery of the Kingdom: the King reigns from a tree. What Rome used to terrify, God used to enthrone. What looked like defeat became victory. What seemed like humiliation became glory.

The cross is not the denial of the Kingdom but its unveiling. And for those who follow, it remains both our hope and our call.

Chapter 9 - Sources

- Hengel, *Crucifixion*, 1977, p. 86.
- Barth, *Church Dogmatics*, IV.1, p. 223.
- Wright, *The Day the Revolution Began*, 2016, p. 358.
- Ladd, *The Presence of the Future*, 1974, p. 193.
- Bonhoeffer, *Letters and Papers from Prison*, 1953, p. 109.
- Wink, *Engaging the Powers*, 1992, p. 151.
- Calvin, *Institutes of the Christian Religion*, II.16.7.
- Bonhoeffer, *Discipleship*, 1937, p. 79.
- Augustine, *City of God*, XIV.28.

Chapter 10

The Early Church and the Kingdom Mission

When Jesus rose from the dead, his followers did not gather around a tomb to reminisce about a noble teacher. They proclaimed a Kingdom. Resurrection was not a metaphor for memory; it was the announcement that God's reign had broken through death itself. From that moment, the early church lived as a Kingdom community, embodying and expanding the reign of God in the world.

Resurrection as the Kingdom's Launch

Luke tells us that the risen Christ spent forty days "speaking about the kingdom of God" (Acts 1:3, NRSVue). His final words echoed the commission of Israel's prophets and the vision of the Psalms: *"You will be my witnesses in Jerusalem, in all Judea and Samaria, and to the ends of the earth"* (Acts 1:8).

N.T. Wright argues that resurrection was not just proof of life after death but "the decisive beginning of God's new creation" (*Surprised by Hope*, 2008, p. 56). The Kingdom had been inaugurated in Jesus' ministry, revealed in the cross, vindicated in resurrection, and now entrusted to the community of disciples.

Pentecost: Spirit and Sovereignty

The Kingdom truly became a movement at Pentecost. Tongues of fire descended, and people from every nation heard the gospel in their own languages (Acts 2:1–11). What Babel had fractured, the Spirit united.

Walter Brueggemann notes that Pentecost "is the radical inversion of imperial speech," where the Spirit dissolves the boundaries that empire exploits (*Theology of the Old Testament*, 1997, p. 645). John Calvin described the Spirit as "the bond by which Christ effectually unites us to himself" (*Institutes*, III.1.1). Pentecost was not simply a religious revival; it was the public enthronement of Christ's reign through his Spirit-filled people.

The Church as Kingdom Community

The book of Acts portrays the early church not as an institution but as a living outpost of the Kingdom. *"They devoted themselves to the apostles' teaching and fellowship, to the breaking of bread and the prayers… all who believed were together and had all things in common"* (Acts 2:42, 44).

Dietrich Bonhoeffer called this "life together," where the presence of Christ is embodied in the community itself (*Life Together*, 1939, p. 21). Ellen Davis highlights the economic dimension: the redistribution of goods was a Kingdom practice of justice, not utopian idealism (*Scripture, Culture, and Agriculture*, 2009, p. 141).

Gustavo Gutiérrez saw in Acts a paradigm of liberation: "The community of believers is called to embody the preferential option for the poor, so that the Kingdom may be good news for all" (*A Theology of Liberation*, 1971, p. 119).

Paul's Gospel of the Kingdom

Paul is often remembered for his doctrine of justification, but his letters are saturated with Kingdom language. *"For the kingdom of God is not food and drink but righteousness and peace and joy in the Holy Spirit"* (Rom 14:17).

George Eldon Ladd emphasized that Paul saw the Kingdom as both present and future: believers are already transferred into the Kingdom of God's Son (Col 1:13), but they also await its final inheritance (1 Cor 15:50) (*The Presence of the Future*, 1974, p. 212).

For Paul, the church was the body of Christ—a community in which Jew and Gentile, slave and free, male and female were one (Gal 3:28). Obery Hendricks Jr. points out that this radical inclusion was political as much as spiritual, dismantling social hierarchies that upheld empire (*The Politics of Jesus*, 2006, p. 88).

Kingdom Against Empire

The early church's proclamation was not safe. To declare "Jesus is Lord" (Rom 10:9) was to declare "Caesar is not." Karl Barth wrote: "The confession of the lordship of Christ is the renunciation of every other lordship" (*Church Dogmatics*, IV.2, p. 112).

Walter Wink reminds us that the church's mission was a confrontation with the Powers—not only spiritual forces but the political, economic, and cultural systems that claimed ultimacy (*Engaging the Powers*, 1992, p. 65). This explains why the early Christians were accused of "turning the world upside down" (Acts 17:6).

The Kingdom Mission Today

The early church was far from perfect. They struggled with divisions, hypocrisy, and compromise. Yet their mission still inspires: they believed the Kingdom was not a distant heaven but a present reality to be lived and shared.

We see the same Kingdom mission whenever churches break bread across divides, share resources in radical generosity, or speak truth to empire. Augustine described the church as a *civitas Dei*, the "city of God" within the city of man, embodying a different order of loyalty and love (*City of God*, XIX.17).

The task is not to replicate Acts as nostalgia but to live its pattern now: Spirit-filled communities of justice, joy, and witness.

Conclusion

The early church carried the Kingdom into the world with boldness and vulnerability. They proclaimed Christ as risen and reigning, they shared their lives in covenant community, they resisted empire's claims, and they bore witness to a new creation.

The Kingdom did not end with Jesus' ascension. It expanded—through Spirit, through community, through witness—to the ends of the earth. And that mission, astonishingly, is now ours.

Chapter 10 - Sources

- Wright, *Surprised by Hope*, 2008, p. 56.
- Brueggemann, *Theology of the Old Testament*, 1997, p. 645.
- Calvin, *Institutes of the Christian Religion*, III.1.1.
- Bonhoeffer, *Life Together*, 1939, p. 21.
- Davis, *Scripture, Culture, and Agriculture*, 2009, p. 141.
- Gutiérrez, *A Theology of Liberation*, 1971, p. 119.
- Ladd, *The Presence of the Future*, 1974, p. 212.
- Hendricks, *The Politics of Jesus*, 2006, p. 88.
- Barth, *Church Dogmatics*, IV.2, p. 112.
- Wink, *Engaging the Powers*, 1992, p. 65.
- Augustine, *City of God*, XIX.17.

Chapter 11

Already and Not Yet

One of the most puzzling yet beautiful aspects of the Kingdom of God is its timing. Has it come already, or is it still to come? The answer in the New Testament is a resounding "yes." The Kingdom is present, and it is future. It is inaugurated but not consummated. It is here, and it is still on the way.

This tension—what theologians call the *eschatological paradox*—is at the heart of Christian discipleship. We live in between.

The Kingdom Already Here

Jesus made bold claims about the present reality of the Kingdom. *"If it is by the finger of God that I cast out demons, then the kingdom of God has come upon you"* (Luke 11:20, NRSVue). In his healings, exorcisms, and table fellowship, the reign of God was not a distant promise but a living reality.

George Eldon Ladd emphasized that "the Kingdom is the reign of God dynamically active among men" (*The Presence of the Future*, 1974, p. 122). Wherever Jesus restored bodies, reconciled sinners, or confronted injustice, the Kingdom was already breaking in.

Paul, too, affirmed this present reality: believers have been "rescued from the power of darkness and transferred into the kingdom of his beloved Son" (Col 1:13). For the early church, the Kingdom was not only awaited but inhabited.

The Kingdom Not Yet Complete

And yet, Jesus also taught his disciples to pray: *"Your kingdom come. Your will be done, on earth as it is in heaven"* (Matt 6:10). If the Kingdom were fully present, such a prayer would be unnecessary.

Paul captured this paradox in Romans 8: creation still groans, believers still wait, redemption is not yet finished. John Goldingay comments: "The Kingdom is both the arrival of God's new order and the stubborn persistence of the old" (*Old Testament Theology*, 2003, p. 377).

Karl Barth put it this way: "We live between the times—the time of Christ's resurrection and the time of his coming again" (*Church Dogmatics*, IV.3.2, p. 310). Hope is not canceled by presence, and presence is not diminished by hope.

Living in the Tension

This paradox has often been misunderstood. Some Christians stress the "already" to the point of triumphalism, assuming the Kingdom is fully here. Others emphasize the "not yet" to the point of resignation, treating the Kingdom as a far-off dream. The New Testament insists on holding both.

Walter Brueggemann argues that this tension creates "a restless hope," where faith resists both despair and complacency (*Hopeful Imagination*, 1986, p. 12). Dallas Willard called it living "in the divine conspiracy," where we participate now in God's reign while still longing for its fullness (*The Divine Conspiracy*, 1998, p. 25).

Theologians of liberation remind us that this paradox is not abstract but practical. Gustavo Gutiérrez writes: "The Kingdom is present in every act of justice, yet history remains unfinished until all oppression ends" (*A Theology of Liberation*, 1971, p. 132).

The Spirit as the Presence of the Future

How do we live in this "in-between time"? The answer is the Holy Spirit. Paul describes the Spirit as the *arrabōn*—the down payment or guarantee of what is to come (2 Cor 1:22; Eph 1:14). The Spirit is both gift and promise: a taste of the future Kingdom now.

John Calvin explained it beautifully: "The Spirit is to us as a kind of spark, which kindles in our hearts the desire for prayer, for the Word, for new life" (*Institutes*, III.1.3). In every act of Spirit-empowered love, we glimpse the coming Kingdom.

Why "Already and Not Yet" Matters

This paradox is not theological trivia. It shapes how we live.

- It keeps us from despair, because the Kingdom is already here.
- It keeps us from arrogance, because the Kingdom is not yet complete.
- It summons us to faithfulness, because our lives are caught between promise and fulfillment.

Augustine once described the Christian life as belonging to "two cities"—the city of God, already known in Christ, and the earthly city, still passing away (*City of God*, XIX.17). To live in both is to live with tension, but also with hope.

Conclusion

The Kingdom of God is already breaking in, yet it is not yet fully realized. This tension is not a flaw in the Gospel but its brilliance. It keeps us awake, longing, participating.

We live in Advent time: Christ has come, Christ is risen, Christ will come again. And between these moments, we pray and work, waiting and witnessing, trusting that the King who has already come will surely come again.

Chapter 11 - Sources

- Ladd, *The Presence of the Future*, 1974, p. 122.
- Goldingay, *Old Testament Theology*, 2003, p. 377.
- Barth, *Church Dogmatics*, IV.3.2, p. 310.
- Brueggemann, *Hopeful Imagination*, 1986, p. 12.
- Willard, *The Divine Conspiracy*, 1998, p. 25.
- Gutiérrez, *A Theology of Liberation*, 1971, p. 132.
- Calvin, *Institutes of the Christian Religion*, III.1.3.
- Augustine, *City of God*, XIX.17.

Chapter 12

Re-centering Our Faith

If we have walked through Scripture with open eyes, the picture should be clear by now: the Kingdom of God is not a marginal theme. It is the thread that weaves creation, covenant, prophets, Jesus, cross, resurrection, and Spirit into a single tapestry. Yet for much of Christian history, this thread has frayed. We have reduced the gospel to personal salvation, privatized faith into individual morality, or postponed hope to a distant heaven. The task before us is to re-center.

The Kingdom as the Gospel's Heart

Jesus did not announce, *"Good news: here's how to get to heaven when you die."* He proclaimed: *"The kingdom of God has come near; repent, and believe in the good news"* (Mark 1:15, NRSVue). N.T. Wright reminds us that this message was not a footnote but the center: "The kingdom of God is what you get when God is running the show" (*Simply Jesus*, 2011, p. 149).

George Eldon Ladd warned that if we neglect the Kingdom, we distort the gospel itself: "The Kingdom is the central theme of the message of Jesus" (*The Gospel of the Kingdom*, 1959, p. 13). The early church understood this. Their proclamation of Jesus as Lord was inseparable from the conviction that God's reign had begun.

The Kingdom as Communal Identity

To re-center on the Kingdom is also to reimagine the church. We are not simply religious consumers or moral individuals; we are a covenant people embodying God's reign together. Luke's portrait in Acts—breaking bread, sharing possessions, praying, bearing witness—is not nostalgia but vocation (Acts 2:42–47).

Dietrich Bonhoeffer captured it in a single phrase: "The church is the church only when it exists for others" (*Letters and Papers from Prison*, 1953, p. 203). Augustine, much earlier, framed it as the distinction between the *civitas Dei* and the *civitas terrena*—a people defined by love of God over love of self (*City of God*, XIX.24).

To live as Kingdom people is to live as a contrast community: generous in a culture of scarcity, forgiving in a culture of vengeance, hopeful in a culture of despair.

The Kingdom as Theological Compass

Re-centering also reshapes theology. Covenant, cross, Spirit, mission—all take on fresh clarity when oriented around the Kingdom. Karl Barth insisted that theology is always proclamation of God's reign in Christ: "The Kingdom of God is the content of the Gospel" (*Church Dogmatics*, IV.3.1, p. 97).

For liberation theologians, this compass points directly toward justice. Gustavo Gutiérrez put it plainly: "The Kingdom is not only about salvation of souls but liberation of human beings in history" (*A Theology of Liberation*, 1971, p. 135). The Kingdom refuses to let theology retreat into abstraction; it insists that God's reign matters here and now.

The Kingdom as Personal Transformation

Of course, re-centering does not bypass the personal. Jesus' call to *repent* is not simply social critique—it is a summons to inner transformation. Dallas Willard described discipleship as "living in the reality of God's Kingdom now" (*The Divine Conspiracy*, 1998, p. xv). This requires a change of heart, a reorientation of desires, a surrender of rival allegiances.

To pray *"your kingdom come"* is to invite God's reign into our daily lives: our work, our relationships, our decisions. Augustine reminded his hearers that God does not reign by force but by love, ruling hearts that freely surrender (*Expositions on the Psalms*, Ps. 96).

A Call to Seek First

So where do we end this first stage of the journey? With the words of Jesus: *"But strive first for the kingdom of God and his righteousness, and all these things will be given to you as well"* (Matt 6:33).

To seek the Kingdom first is not to ignore the realities of daily life—food, clothing, shelter—but to trust that when God reigns, these things fall into place. It is to make the Kingdom our compass, our center, our aim.

Walter Brueggemann calls this a summons to "imagine the world differently," not as Pharaoh or Caesar would have it, but as God intends (*The Prophetic Imagination*, 1978, p. 67). It is an invitation into hope, risk, and joy.

Conclusion: Re-centering Our Faith

The Kingdom of God is not a distant dream or a theological abstraction. It is the reality Jesus proclaimed, embodied, and entrusted to us. To re-center our faith around the Kingdom is to remember creation's purpose, covenant's calling, the prophets' hope, Jesus' ministry, the cross's paradox, resurrection's victory, and the Spirit's presence.

It is to live in the tension of already and not yet, to be shaped as a Kingdom community, and to participate in God's mission of justice, mercy, and reconciliation.

The question now is simple, though never easy: will we seek first the Kingdom?

Chapter 12 - Sources

- Wright, *Simply Jesus*, 2011, p. 149.
- Ladd, *The Gospel of the Kingdom*, 1959, p. 13.
- Bonhoeffer, *Letters and Papers from Prison*, 1953, p. 203.
- Augustine, *City of God*, XIX.24.
- Barth, *Church Dogmatics*, IV.3.1, p. 97.
- Gutiérrez, *A Theology of Liberation*, 1971, p. 135.
- Willard, *The Divine Conspiracy*, 1998, p. xv.
- Augustine, *Expositions on the Psalms*, Ps. 96.
- Brueggemann, *The Prophetic Imagination*, 1978, p. 67.

Epilogue

A Forward Glance

We have traced the Kingdom of God from the first pages of Genesis to the life of the early church. We have seen creation as the King's temple, covenant as the charter of a Kingdom people, prophets as the fierce memory of God's reign, and Jesus as the one who announced and embodied the Kingdom. We have stood at the cross, paradoxically a throne, and we have watched resurrection and Spirit-filled community declare that the Kingdom is already here, though not yet complete.

And if all of this feels like standing at the edge of something vast—that's because it is.

The Kingdom is not simply a doctrine to memorize or a theme to admire. It is a reality pressing in on us, reshaping our imagination, demanding our allegiance. It is not "over there," in someone else's story. It is here, in ours.

But this story is not finished. Book 1 has been about *foundations*—laying the groundwork, listening to the voices of Scripture, seeing the Kingdom unfold across covenant, prophets, and promise. In Book 2, we turn our eyes more fully to Jesus. For if the Kingdom is the melody of Scripture, then Jesus is the song made flesh.

He will tell stories, heal the broken, challenge the powers, and gather a community that lives by a new order. And he will show us, in ways that still confound and transform, what it means to say: *The Kingdom of God has come near.*

As we move forward, I invite you to keep asking the simplest and most disruptive of questions: What does it mean—in my time, in my place—to live as though God truly reigns?

Because that question is where theology becomes discipleship, where history becomes hope, and where the Kingdom ceases to be just a word and becomes our life.

Blessings - Pastor Mick Finch

www.ingramcontent.com/pod-product-compliance
Lightning Source LLC
Chambersburg PA
CBHW051334120626
46547CB00016B/2534